KIAC.

MAR   2018

BETWEEN TWO DOGS

BETWEEN TWO DOGS

SHAINA FISHMAN

Skyhorse Publishing

To my parents, for always having a house full of animals:

Tigger
Willie
Tova
Alex
Tammy
Yoni
Heidi
Boots
Jinjy
Blue
Woody
and Cosmo

INTRODUCTION

What is between two dogs? Sometimes it is affection. Sometimes friendship. Sometimes indifference or anger. Sometimes love. Every relationship between dogs, just like every relationship between people, is unique. Exploring the relationships between dogs was the inspiration for this book.

Growing up in a household that had at least two cats and two dogs at any given time, I had the privilege to watch relationships between animals unfold. As a young girl, I adopted a kitten and named him Yoni. He was the most energized member of the household and forced the other cats and dogs to become his playmates. But as Yoni grew older, he lost interest in playing with the other animals. Even when two new dogs joined the family and wanted to play with him, he had no interest. Then, when Yoni was fifteen years old, Cosmo the Papillon was brought into the mix, and the playful kitten in Yoni was reignited. Cosmo would run circles around the ottoman as Yoni sat on it, pawing at him and teasing him. The renewed playfulness in that old cat was an eye-opener. He hadn't wanted to play with the other dogs, but he allowed Cosmo to be his playmate. Why was the relationship between Yoni and Cosmo different? Reflecting on their unique relationship inspired me to want to understand more about the connections between animals. I would later become a professional animal photographer, but my path was not a direct route.

I studied commercial photography at Syracuse University, intent on becoming a fashion photographer. After college, I began my career in New York City, working as a digital tech for some of the best fashion photographers in the industry with top models and A-list celebrities on glamorous shoots. Yet, even though I was getting an up-close look at the career that I came to New York to pursue, I was not inspired to shoot. I carried my camera with me everywhere, but for months did not find anything I wanted to photograph.

Most nights, after a day on a fashion shoot, I brought Cosmo and my camera to the Madison Square Park dog run. One evening at the dog run, I was finally inspired to capture some images; I photographed Cosmo and other dogs playing, running, and wrestling. I shot these interactions on black-and-white film and had to wait days to see what I'd shot. When I finally got back from the lab, the processed film images were filled with joy, humor, and playfulness. Never before had I felt so much excitement for something I had photographed. Later, while reviewing what I had captured that evening and on many subsequent visits to the dog park, I realized that my interest and skill was in photographing animals.

Since those early days at the dog run, and for the past ten years, I have worked to create images that depict dogs with discernible emotions so that people can relate to the animals. Every dog has a unique personality and with that comes distinct traits and idiosyncrasies. I aim to capture the range of dogs' expressions to convey an emotion that we humans can recognize. Dogs can be more than just cute beings; they can have emotional depth. I want people to form a connection with the dogs in my images.

For this book, I took my aspirations one step further by pairing dogs together to explore how they interact. What transpired between the dogs was a plethora of dynamic relationships. When dogs entered my studio for their shoots for this book, they were ÿooded with stimuli: new people interested in playing with them, smells from past visitors, strange-looking equipment, and tons of space to claim as their own. I think most dogs believed the studio was some kind of strange dog park. Almost all of the dogs were eager to play and explore the new and exciting space.

The corgi puppies, Edison and Dallas, came into the studio with a burst of energy. They ran in circles and chased each other by sliding on the glossy ÿoor and knocking into one another as their paths crossed. They were so caught up in their play that they didn't care about the camera and lights. I corralled their play session to capture their folly. Since they didn't pay attention to the space around them and just wanted to play with each other, the challenge of photographing these playmates was keeping them on the set.

Completely opposite the corgis were the pugs. Nena, the adult, did not care to incorporate Jack, the pug puppy, into her moment in the spotlight. Jack wanted constant physical contact with Nena and would try to curl up next to her, but she paid no attention to him and went about her routine: sit, lay down, roll over, claim a treat, and repeat. As long as Jack didn't get in the way of her spotlight, she tolerated his presence. Once Nena was tired and full of treats, Jack was able to snuggle up to her for a nap.

These are just two stories of the relationships I observed while photographing dogs for this book. This project sought to capture the relationship between pairs of dogs—and not only each dog's emotional range, but also the humorous and endearing moments between each pair. I hope the images make you smile and laugh and that they reveal to you what is between the two dogs.

THE DOGS

Pugs
Nena: 3 years
Jack: 13 weeks
Nena loves her stuffed toys; she won't leave the house without one in her mouth. She steals toys from Jack to engage him in a tug-of-war match or start a game of chase. Despite the attempts by Nena, Jack just wants to snuggle and be sweet.

Basset Hounds
Cyan Pepper: 12 weeks
Jalapeno Popper: 12 weeks
Winning over Pepper and Popper is easily done with a belly rub. They love receiving a good massage and an exorbitant amount of treats. Their ears are best left alone since they are very sensitive. When playing, biting anywhere on the body is fair game except for the ears.

English Springer Spaniels
Bella: 4 years
Nessie: 7 weeks
Bella and Nessie are famous for winning people over with their soft and sweet expressions. If their pleading eyes and sad faces don't win your heart, their affection and eagerness to please will. They hate being ignored by humans or dogs and will paw and bark until they receive a reaction.

American Eskimos

Atka: 10 years

Kayu: 5 months

Both Atka and Kayu know a multitude of tricks and perform in shows for children and veterans. They visit military bases and nursing homes and comfort those in need as therapy dogs.

Bulldogs

Emily Rose: 4 years

Tycoon: 14 weeks

Emily and Tycoon are self-proclaimed lap dogs. Despite their laid-back personalities, they quickly transform from mushes to playful clowns. They spend summers frolicking in a kiddie pool and rolling around in the grass to escape the dog days of summer. Bulldogs are notorious for disliking the heat.

Cavalier King Charles Spaniels

Romeo: 3 years

Pete: 12 weeks

Cavaliers are mostly a docile and calm breed. They are known to be devoted and loyal companions. Romeo and Pete's favorite activity is a good snuggle, but they don't shy away from playing with one another or engaging with people in a game of fetch.

Chihuahuas

Twee: 4 years

Max: 13 weeks

Max and Twee's happiness is contagious. When Max gets the zoomies—a burst of energy that gets him running around the room—it's hard not to laugh at the antics. The scene of the darting, unstoppable puppy amuses even the stoic Twee.

Corgis

Edison: 9 weeks

Dallas: 9 weeks

Edison and Dallas love playing. They pull each other's tail and chew on each other's ears. Neither puppy is the least bit timid or shy. Despite the rambunctiousness, they are both sweet and biddable.

Shorthaired Dachshunds

Huckleberry: 2 years

Olive: 8 weeks

Olive is a typical puppy and loves pestering Huckleberry. She will do all she can to get him to play with her. It doesn't take much to get Huckleberry to engage in a wrestling match since he too loves to cavort.

French Bulldogs

Walter: 2 years
Vence: 10 weeks
Walter is older, but just as, if not more, playful than Vence. Like typical French bulldogs, when playing they both grunt and snort. Their appearance along with the noises has given this breed the affectionate nickname of "pigdog."

Dalmatians

Elizabeth: 8 weeks
Cece: 8 weeks
Dalmatians are born all white and get their spots a couple weeks later. Cece and Elizabeth got their spots early when the owner's young daughter, unwilling to wait, took to them with a permanent marker. Like the antics with the marker, they too are mischievous and get themselves into predicaments.

Portuguese Water Dogs

Sky: 10 weeks
Gregg: 10 weeks
The Allman Brothers Band inspired the names for these puppies. Sky and Gregg are rambunctious and playful puppies, but also are wildly obedient and intelligent. They can go from carefree and frisky to attentive and stoic in a moment.

Pomeranians

Melody: 4 years
Buddy: 4 months
Buddy loves companionship. He got his name when he was a puppy and wouldn't eat until a friend joined him to share the meal. He waited by his bowl until a buddy showed up. Melody provides the companionship he so craves.

Longhaired Dachshunds

Hazelnut: 2 years
Blackberry: 8 weeks
Hazelnut, or Hazel for short, loves people, especially children. When meeting someone new, she will lay on her back, allowing and expecting belly rubs. Blackberry is influenced by Hazel's eagerness for belly rubs and exhibits the same behavior.

Boston Terriers

Tabatha: 4 years
Bowie: 14 weeks
Haggerty spots are rumored to be a sign of good luck, and both Tabatha and Bowie have the marking, common with Boston Terriers, on the top of their head. For them, with the good luck came a friskiness. They both love to wrestle and chew on one another's ears while making comical grunting noises.

Jack Russell Terriers

Ivy: 18 months
London: 12 weeks

Ivy and London will do anything and go anywhere as long as it is together. They are loving companions to each other and to people. Individually, they thrive at agility. Their favorite obstacles are the bridges and tunnels. Their least desired activity is being groomed. Lucky for them, they don't require much primping.

Great Pyrenees

Carly: 11 weeks
Smokey: 11 weeks

Great Pyrenees are easily mistaken for polar bears, but much more willing to snuggle. Carly and Smokey are all fluff and affection. They love children and have an innate desire to protect them. The breed has been working for hundreds of years with shepherds to protect sheep and other animal flocks.

Golden Retrievers

Cash: 3 years
Buttercup: 8 weeks

Cash loves giving hugs to people and grooming the puppy. Buttercup doesn't mind all the affection and attention. Both dogs have a unique, beautiful coat and infectious, adorable smiles.

Norwich Terriers

Wren: 2½ years
Cleo: 9 weeks

These little Norwich terriers aren't afraid of anything. Wren and Cleo don't let their small size get in the way of getting into mischief. Their favorite pastimes are chasing rodents and bird-watching. The bird feeder outside their window provides constant entertainment.

German Shepherds

Petey: 2 years, 8 months
Huey: 4 months

Huey always manages to irritate Petey with his puppy antics. Like most puppies, Huey always wants to wrestle and rumble. Despite Petey's shyness, Huey wins him over with his outgoing and friendly rowdiness.

Miniature Pinschers

Mr. Bojangles: 9 years
Tiny Dancer: 6 months

No tail is safe from Tiny; she will playfully swat and bite any tail encountered. Bojangles is the frequent recipient of such experiences. If a tail biting doesn't get a reaction from Bojangles, Tiny does whatever it takes to be acknowledged and start a rumble.

Huskies

Stella: 18 months

Gidget: 8 weeks

Stella and Gidget do not like heat. They thrive in the winter months when they can go for long runs. Stella will soon teach Gidget the skill and joy of pulling a sled.

Australian Shepherds

Hazel: 1 year

Riley: 10 months

Despite their name, Australian shepherds originated in the United States. The breed has a natural herding instinct, which makes for a lively household with sprightly play. Hazel and Riley are both full of energy and exceptionally intelligent.

French Bulldogs

Ula: 3 years

Ollie: 15 weeks

Ula's name is short for *ohh la la,* and Ollie is short for Oliver. Their favorite snack is peanut butter, and they enjoy it while engaging in their favorite activity, watching television. Their favorite programs are ones that feature animals.

Rhodesian Ridgebacks

Hazelnut: 3 years
Leo: 8 weeks
Rhodesian ridgebacks are independent dogs. That independence oftentimes gets mislabeled as stubbornness. But Hazelnut and Leo are undoubtedly both independent and stubborn. Don't try to get either of them to do anything he doesn't want to without the involvement of treats.

Miniature Beagles

Pearl: 3 years
Tiny: 8 months
Both Pearl and Tiny are happy dogs. Pearl is gentle, serene, and sweet. Tiny is a ball of energy and doesn't stop moving. They could not be more opposite. Their common characteristic is that they both love playing with kittens.

Labs

Shlep: 4 years
Hintele: 4 months
Shlep and Hintele love being petted and hate when anyone stops giving them attention. Shlep, which means "to carry something heavy" in Yiddish, got his name when he was a puppy. He would lie down halfway through walks and have to be dragged the rest of the way home.

Beagles

Gerald: 2 years

Paden: 7 weeks

Paden is the perfectly balanced mix of sleepy and hyperactive. When awake, he is all about stealing treats and getting affection. While nodding off to sleep, his focus is snuggling with Gerald. His love for treats came from Gerald, whose sole motivation is food.

German Shorthaired Pointers

Ceilidh: 7 years

Rae: 7 weeks

Ceilidh and Rae are the perfect match. Both of their best talents are cuddling. Ceilidh is affectionate and gentle with all puppies, even when barrages of them climb all over her. The puppies can also count on her to be an equitable playmate. Rae loves chasing her around the yard.

Chocolate Labs

Seadoo: 11 weeks

Kawasaki: 11 weeks

Seadoo and Kawasaki are easily mistaken for vacuum cleaners; they eat any food or crumb in sniffing range. Despite their invaluable assistance in keeping their home clean, they were named after Jet Skis. They don't ride the Jet Skis, but they love the water.

ACKNOWLEDGMENTS

Photographing one dog by itself can be a test in patience, but photographing two dogs together is a whole other feat. There are many people who helped make this book a reality.

A big hug and thank-you to my husband, Ryan Finkel, for his advice, support, encouragement, and humor throughout the creation of this book.

To my dad and mom, Leslie and Susie, for their unwavering love, which that allows me to always follow my ambitions.

Thank you to my editor, Julia Abramoff, for seeing the potential in me to create this book.

Thank you to Lori Cannava for not only her amazing retouching, but also for always being available for a late-night pep talk and for being an incredible friend.

The images in this book were captured at Go Studios. I owe an abundance of gratitude to its owner, Halley Ganges, for his support and putting up with the barking dogs and piles of animal hair. Also, to Kevin Goon for providing the best equipment and for understanding that animals have accidents.

Thanks to my agents, Ralph Mennemeyer and Dianne Morales of M Represents, who continually impress me with their newfound knowledge and appreciation of dogs.

To my friends Kate Mason and Nicolette Marinos for enduring my constant sharing of dog images. Your advice and views were a valuable resource.

Thank you to my assistants, Mike Broussard and Roeg Cohen, for going the extra step, sweeping up dog hair, and wiping off drool. It's a dirty job, but the plus side is snuggling with all the cutest dogs.

Thanks to Linda Hanrahan for her tireless work in bringing together these incredible dog pairs. I appreciate your dedication to the project.

And finally, thank you to all the dog owners and handlers who were a part of this project. Every person and dog was a delight to work with. Thank you, Thy Cavagnaro, Annie Wasserman, Susan Gural, Rita Wagoner, Stephanie Teed, Simon Goldin, Carolyn McGarry, Patty Mitchell, Jill Kiernan, Sue Lucatorto, Kimberlee Young, Tracey Monahan, Donald Snyder, Patricia Sulzberger, Jamie Oliva, Sheryl Schulze, Andrew Kalmanash, Irene and Drew Rabinowitz, Cathy Iacopelli, Barbara and Doug Kahl, Lisa M. Hoffman, Sharon and Henry Scully, Sue Sobel, Jane O'Halloran, Ada Nieves, Linda Anthony, Jerrie Champlin, Bob Baranowski, Jean Buscaglia-Yurkiewicz, Betty McDonnell, and Rick Busda.